And Pretend

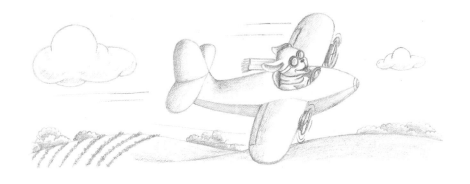

By
Pamela Conn Beall and Susan Hagan Nipp

Illustrated by
Nancy Spence Klein

PSS!
PRICE STERN SLOAN

THE LAND OF SILLY

Susan Nipp, Adapted

Traditional

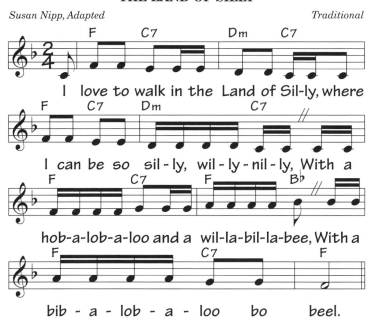

I love to walk in the Land of Sil-ly, where

I can be so sil - ly, wil - ly - nil - ly, With a

hob-a-lob-a-loo and a wil-la-bil-la-bee, With a

bib - a - lob - a - loo   bo   beel.

F

Shool, shool, shool I rool,

C7 **F** **C7**

Shool I shag-a-rack shool-a-bob-a-loo, In the

F **Bb**

Land of Sil-ly with a nil-ly wil-ly we, With a

F **C7** **F**

bib - a - lob - a - loo bo beel.

5

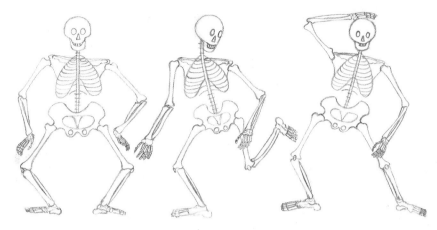

BONES

My bones make up my skeleton,
Which is the frame of me,
And though you cannot see them,
My bones move easily.

For I can leap and twist and creep
And run and sway and jiggle
And bend and slide and hop and glide
And bounce and roll and wiggle.

Susan Nipp

(Saint-Saëns: *Danse Macabre* — 1875)

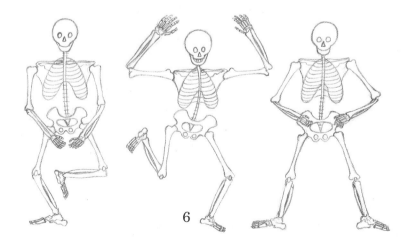

I'M A CLOWN

Susan Nipp   *Traditional*

1. I'm a clown! Honk! Honk!

I'm a clown! Honk! Honk!

Jug - gl - ing, jug - gl - ing, toss the balls,

Strug - gl - ing, strug - gl - ing as they fall,

7

Tum-bl-ing, stum-bl-ing, fum-bl-ing, mum-bl-ing,

Catch   the   balls.

2. I'm a clown! *Honk! Honk!*
   I'm a clown! *Honk! Honk!*
   Somersault, somersault, over I go,
   Over and round on the ground I go,
   Down on the ground going over and round
   From my head to toe.

3. I'm a clown! *Honk! Honk!*
   I'm a clown! *Honk! Honk!*
   Balancing, balancing on the wire,
   High on the wire, so I must not tire,
   Tipping and dipping and slipping and tripping while
   On the wire.

I'm a cowboy and this is my horse, Old Paint.

All right, Old Paint, I'll brush you down a bit.

Here, have some oats.

Now, I'll put on the saddle.

Hold still, boy, while I get on.

All right, Old Paint, let's start walking down the trail.

OLD TEXAS

Traditional

1. I'm goin' to leave _____ old __ Tex-as now, They've got no use _____ __ for the long - horned cow. _____

2. The hard, hard ground will be my bed,
   And the saddle seat will hold my head.

9

Okay, Old Paint, let's trot along a bit faster.

THE OLD CHISHOLM TRAIL

Traditional

1. Oh, come a-long boys and lis-ten to my tale,

I'll tell you of my trou-bles on the old Chis-holm Trail,

Chorus
Sing-in' ki - yi yip-pi yip-pi yay, yip-pi yay!

Sing - in' ki - yi yip-pi yip-pi yay! _____

2. I'm up in the mornin' before daylight,
   And before I sleep, the moon shines bright.

   (Chorus)

Ready, Old Paint? Let's gallop!

(Rossini: *William Tell Overture* — 1829)

10

THE LAND OF SLOW MOTION

Susan Nipp   *Susan Nipp*

Verse F G7 C

1. I'm wak-ing up in the Land of Slow Mo-tion,

G7 C

Land of Slow Mo-tion, Land of Slow Mo-tion, I'm

F G7 C

wak - ing up in the Land of Slow Mo-tion and

Dm G7 C

I   can   bare - ly   move.

11

(Chorus—spoken slowly)
I get out of bed...
And brush my teeth...
Put on my clothes...
And have something to eat...

I run outside...
And play catch with my brother...
I ride my bike...
Then swim with my sister...

I jump over rocks...
And climb a tree...
Then run back home...
And eat with my family...

I put on my pajamas...
And brush my teeth...
I go to bed...
And fall right to sleep.

(Verse—quickly)
2. I'm waking up in the Land of Fast Motion,
   Land of Fast Motion, Land of Fast Motion,
   I'm waking up in the Land of Fast Motion,
   And I can hardly stop.

   (Repeat chorus—spoken quickly)

12

Around the house, there are all kinds of things that move. Can you move like they do?

OH, WHEN

Susan Nipp, Pam Beall

Traditional

1. Oh, when the clothes wash in the wash-er, Oh, when the clothes wash in the wash-er, Oh, how they slish and slosh in the wash-er,_____ When the clothes wash in the wash-er.

13

2. Oh, when the clothes dry in the dryer,
   Oh, when the clothes dry in the dryer,
   Oh, how they tumble, tumble, tumble in the dryer,
   When the clothes dry in the dryer.

3. Oh, when the juice twirls in the blender,
   Oh, when the juice twirls in the blender,
   Oh, how it twirls and swirls in the blender,
   When the juice twirls in the blender.

4. Oh, when the corn pops in the popper,
   Oh, when the corn pops in the popper,
   Oh, how it pops and pops in the popper,
   When the corn pops in the popper.

What is that in the middle of the sidewalk?

A ROCK BLOCKS THE WALK

Susan Nipp   *Traditional*

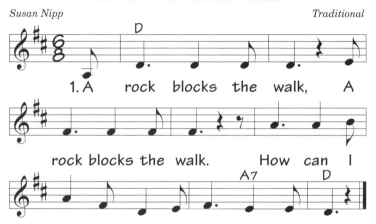

1. A rock blocks the walk, A rock blocks the walk. How can I move the thing? A rock blocks the walk.

2. I push on the rock,
   I push on the rock.
   How can I move the thing?
   I push on the rock.

15

3. I pull on the rock,
   I pull on the rock.
   How can I move the thing?
   I pull on the rock.

4. I walk round the rock,
   I walk round the rock,
   I cannot move the thing,
   So, I walk round the rock on the block.

A WALK THROUGH THE FOREST

One day little Chipper Chipmunk peeked through my window. He blinked at me as though asking me to play. I hurried outside to find him and he began to scamper away.

We ran through the meadow.
(Vivaldi: *Flute Concerto in G Minor,* "*LaNotte,*" *Allegro* — 1731)

We skipped down the forest trail.
(Rimsky-Korsakov: *Alborado* from *Cappriccio Espagnol* — 1892

We balanced on a log over the rushing stream.
(Sibelius: *Finlandia* — 1899)

We tiptoed past sleeping Mr. Porcupine.
(Bach: *Air on G String* from *Suite No. 3 in D* — 1727)

We hopped around the trees with Missy Rabbit.
(Tchaikovsky: *Polonaise* from *Eugene Onegin* — 1878)

We twirled with the leaves as they fell from the trees.
(Grieg: *Morning* from *Peer Gynt* — 1876)

17

We helped the ants carry their heavy picnic baskets slowly to the sandy beach.

(Elgar: *Pomp and Circumstance, March No. 1* — 1901)

After the picnic, we played and danced with the ants.

(Bizet: *Les Toreadors* from *Carmen* — 1875)

We waved good-bye to the ants and continued down the path.

We came to a dark tunnel and crawled through it.

(Handel: *Largo* from *Xerxes* — 1734)

I came out of the tunnel and couldn't find Chipper. What happened? I went to look for him.

(Beethoven: *Symphony No. 5, 1st Movement* — 1885)

Hooray! I found him playfully hiding behind a bush. We laughed and called our forest friends to join us as we danced wildly.

(J. Strauss II: *Tritsch Tratsch Polka* — 1858)

As we thought about our wonderful day, we happily marched back home.

(Purcell: *Trumpet Tune* — 1685)

Susan Nipp

Inside a box, I'm scrunched up tight,
I do not move 'til the music's right.

JACK-IN-THE-BOX

Susan Nipp   *Traditional*

1. My name is Jack-in-the-Box, I love to hide from you, I qui-et-ly stay in-side the box, 'Til POP! I sur-prise you.

2. Down I go back into my box
   To hide again from you,
   I quietly stay inside the box,
   'Til POP! I surprise you.

MY BLUE BALLOON

Susan Nipp   *Susan Nipp*

I have a blue bal-loon in my pock-et,   I

have a blue bal-loon in   my pock-et,   I'll

show it to you, ___ It's ti-ny, that's true, ___

But   it   can   get   real - ly   big.

Whoo, *(blowing)* _____ whoo, _____ whoo, _____

whoo,_____ Whew! Tie a knot!

Oops! Watch out! Try again!

Whoo,_____ whoo,_____ whoo,_____

whoo,_____ Whew! Tie a knot!

Float-ing, float-ing, my big blue bal - loon,

Float-ing, float-ing, my big blue bal - loon,

Swirl-ing and twirl-ing and whirl-ing a-round, My

big blue bal - loon in the air._____

It's floating down! POP!

21

I'M A TOP

Susan Nipp

Susan Nipp

I'm a top, spin-n-n! Spin, spin,

spin, I'm a top and I spin all a - round,

Spin, spin, spin, I'm a top and I

spin all a - round, Spin-ning and spin-ning and

spin-ning a - round, Spin-ning and spin-ning, I

start to slow down, When I slow

down, then I start once a - gain, Fast - er and

fast-er and fast-er I spin-n-n! Plop!

THE TOY SHOP AT MIDNIGHT

The toys in the toy shop are silent all day,
But when it is midnight, they all start to play.

The little tin soldier marches quite stiffly...
(Herbert: *March of the Toys* from *Babes in Toyland* — 1903)

The fluffy old rag doll flops as she walks...
(Vivaldi: *The Four Seasons, Autumn; Allegro* — 1725)

The small ballerina twirls on her toes...
(Tchaikovsky: *Waltz of the Flowers* from *The Nutcracker* — 1892)

The mechanical robot moves with a jerk...
(Debussy: *Golliwogg's Cakewalk* from *Children's Corner* — 1908)

The big, cuddly teddy bear dances quite clumsily...
(Tchaikovsky: *Piano Concerto No. 1 in B Flat minor, 1st Movement* — 1875)

But just as the sun starts to peek o'er the hill,
The toys take their places and once more are still.
(Grieg: *Morning* from *Peer Gynt* — 1876)

Susan Nipp

24

THE ORCHESTRA

sings, _____ la, la, _____ la, ___ la.

clar - i - net goes doo-dle, doo-dle, doo-dle det.

trum - pet, ta - ta- ta - ta-ta - ta-ta-ta-ta - ta.

bone _____ says doo _____ wah.

boom, boom, boom, boom, boom, boom.

MARCH

Attention!
March in place, 2, 3, 4!
Left, right, left, right, left, right, left!
Forward...march, 2, 3, 4,
1, 2, 3, 4!

To the left...march!

To the right...march!

To the rear...march!

Attention, 2, 3, 4,
1, 2, 3, 4,
Ready...stop!

(John Philip Sousa: *The Stars and Stripes Forever* — 1897)

28

ROCK BAND

Susan Nipp   *Susan Nipp*

Rock-in' and a - roll-in' in   my rock band,__

Rock-in' and a - roll-in' in   my rock band,__

Rock-in' and a - roll - in' in   my rock band,__

Oh,____   let's   rock.____

Let's hear the 'lec - tric gui - tar,__   *(guitar)*

30